MrQuickPick's 1-2-3 Business Plan to Unlocking Cars for Profit!

The Step-by-Step Guide to Make Money Now as a Mobile Locksmith and Roadside Services Provider

By Jon Taylor

MrQuickPick USA

Did you ever wonder how much the person who just unlocked your car actually makes for a living?
He just charged you $60 for what seemed like thirty seconds of actual work, but surely he doesn't keep all of that, or does he?

He must have overhead, storefront, expensive equipment and years of training? Maybe... Or just maybe he works from home, out of his car, with minimal tools and training, advertising online while pocketing $200-$300+ per day, every day, all week long.

Perhaps he's knocking down six-figures a year, driving around town providing roadside services to other people who are trying to get to their "real" jobs (working for someone else).

Find out how one guy quit the 9-5 world to start his own lockout business and ended up grossing over half a million dollars in his first three years, with no more mechanical experience or training than the next "suit and tie" office guy...Meet MrQuickPick!

Contents:

THE AUTHOR

Meet Jon Taylor, MrQuickPick

While working as a hotel general manger, Jon would often assist guests with their automotive needs, calling on auto clubs to help with a tire change, dead battery or keys locked in a car. Sometimes it would take so long for help to arrive that he would simply grab some tools and do it himself. That's when he realized he could put his own business savvy and strong work ethic into starting and running his own "lock & road" service.

His first company, Quick Pick Lockout Service, would gross **over half a million dollars in its first three years** and, in the process, win AAA's prestigious Member's Choice Award for three consecutive years. Jon has since taken his model for success and helped fellow entrepreneurs get into business for themselves as **MrQuickPick** licensees, right in their own hometowns!

"I am totally convinced that ANYONE with a reliable vehicle and a cell phone can start their own successful lockout and roadside assistance business, just like I did, and now I'm going to show you how. Veterans, including Military, Police, Fire, First Responders (even with disability) this means you too! Whether you want to run the business AND do the work or just run the business and hire contractors to do the rest, we'll cover all the bases to starting and operating your own profitable business.

These are the same steps and procedures **MrQuickPick** used in setting up the first "Lock and Road Service", including the good (what worked well), the bad (what didn't work so well) and the ugly (what you really want to avoid). From valuable ideas (did you even realize you could sign up to receive "jobs" from the major auto clubs?) to expensive lessons, we'll share them with you, step-by-step, in plain English... no fluffy words... no convoluted explanations. Just the cold, hard facts... now let's get this business started!"

"Jon has excelled as a "lockout specialist" for AAA. His company has received numerous awards for their great service. AAA members were totally satisfied!"

Bob Hollifield, President and CEO (Retired) AAA KY.

Right this very minute, someone has locked their keys in their car. It happens every day, in every city across the nation (including yours), all day long and into the wee hours of the morning. And it's not just keys locked inside a car. Drivers across America are constantly in need of jump starts, tire changes, gas delivery and lockout service. The demand is there. The skills are there (come on now, almost anyone can jump start a car or deliver gas, even change a tire or unlock a car with a little training).

Where are you? At a low paying 9-5? Suit and tie? Or maybe you're looking for a job, a better job or in between jobs? Perhaps you're just getting out of the military, maybe even a disabled veteran (as I am), trying to transition back into the civilian world.

If you've always wanted to be your own boss and you're not afraid of a little hard work, maybe it's time to ditch the suit and tie, or put the "help wanted" search on hold. Maybe, just maybe, lockout service and roadside assistance (or what we like to call "Lock & Road Service") is right for you. The demand is there and the skills are there, now you just need the plan!

THE PLAN

I have always wanted to start my own business...

In fact, I've "almost" started many!

There was the one where I was going to change out parking lot lights with a boom truck (very expensive startup, high liability), on-call hotel maintenance (heavy competition, expensive marketing), webpage design (competition, little experience), senior care assistance (competition, marketing issues, liability), hotel video advertising (marketing issues, low return on investment/ROI).

Trust me, I could go on. Many ideas, some very good, but always an obstacle; be it financial, experience or competition/low ROI. That all changed in August of 2006. One of my associates at the hotel I managed told me he had taken on a part-time job in the evenings with a local locksmith company (btw, he and I had looked into starting a travel and tour guide business months earlier with many of the above mentioned obstacles). James called me one evening and said "you've got to see this". He threw his keys in his car, locked the door and within seconds he had unlocked the vehicle and retrieved his keys. We tried it with my car and... the same quick result. People all over town were calling to have their cars and trucks (and houses and businesses) unlocked and paying $50, $60, $70+ a pop! The actual job was so quick and easy, it was as if people were calling up and saying "hey, can you come on over and pick up this crisp $50 bill I have for you?" Sure no problem! But could we actually do this ourselves? What about the past obstacles such as start up costs, experience, ROI and competition?

Start up costs:

Tools – a very good yet very basic lockout kit with everything we would need to get into most any vehicle was only around $70. Another $100 got us some specialty tools and backup equipment. That was it! We did the math: 20 lockouts per today at $40 each equals $800 per day. Not bad! We originally did not plan on the other roadside assistance aspects of this job (tire changes, jump starts, etc). It was only after we started out with only one or two lockouts a day that we decided we needed to add to our repertoire. So... additional tools for the other roadside assistance tasks added about another $200. So we're in for around $400 in tools. No storefront or office required. We would work right from our homes using our cell phones and personal vehicles. About $200 worth of vinyl car lettering (optional) and my startup costs were now at about $600.

Experience:

More "practice" than God-given talent! I had never used a lockout tool until starting this business. In fact, most of my training ended up being "on the job". There are numerous resources online (we have provided some links in the "Services" chapter), and auto lockout manuals with step-by-step unlock procedures for every year, make and model are readily available.

For real life, hands-on training you can spend an afternoon at the local auto salvage yard. There you can unlock cars until your heart's content, with no worries of scratching someone's paint job or breaking a window. Unlock fifty cars and trucks of different years, makes and models and I'd say you're as well (if not better) trained than most of your competition!

*Please Note: I am not a locksmith and I do not claim to be a locksmith. The business of unlocking vehicles is unregulated in most states. In others you must be licensed, such as in Virginia where lockout service and locksmiths are regulated by the Department of Criminal Justice (DCJS).

Return on investment (ROI):

The ROI for this type of business can be incredible. Start-up costs for the tools were right around $400. You're working from home so there is no office or shop to lease (in fact, you can claim a percentage of your home as a business expense on your taxes!). You can also claim your mileage at the end of the year (55.5 cents per mile for 2012) which can be a pretty big deduction when you average around 40,000 miles per year ($22,200). Marketing will be your biggest expense in this business, so what you spend to make the phone ring can make or break your bottom line (another good reason for adding the auto clubs, as those jobs cost you nothing in marketing).

Competition:

If you look in the business opportunity magazines there is only one "true" national company in this business. I say "true" because there are many "national looking" companies online with flashy websites, but they are nothing more than a middleman. They advertise a very low price upfront only to raise it once they arrive. They are often the focus of undercover investigations. They try to recruit local locksmiths and charge a fee to provide leads. This would only drive up your costs and, in turn, your pricing. Stay away from these scam artists at all costs. You can do your own marketing! Other than the one national company there are typically a handful of local "mom-and-pop" companies, so it pretty much boils down to "the best marketing gets the calls".

THE BUSINESS - DEFINED

What exactly is "Lock and Road Service" anyway?

There are actually two parts to the business:

1. **The Lockout Service** – You are unlocking cars and trucks (and houses if you can) as XYZ Inc. (your own business). You are advertising your services and receiving calls right to your cell phone. You may expand your offerings to include traditional lock and locksmith work, such as making keys.
   a. The Pros: You are in complete control of pricing the jobs; you can charge whatever the market will bear.
   b. The Cons: You are paying for your own advertising so you better know what you're doing, especially when using pay-per-click (Google Adwords) advertising.
2. **The Roadside Assistance** -You are signed up as a Service Provider with various, national auto clubs and receive calls to perform light-duty services within a designated area (about a 20 mile radius of your base address). These light-duty services include jump starts, tire changes, lockouts and fluid delivery (gas/diesel) to cars, SUVs, and pick-up trucks (nothing big like semi's or dump trucks, unless you want to add these medium and heavy duty services, or even towing).
   a. The Pros: You don't pay for any advertising. You don't pay the auto clubs for calls (they pay you). You are signed up as an independent contractor, working for yourself.
   b. The Cons: The clubs set the prices they are willing to pay you, typically lower than you would charge.

Why not just setup the lockout service and forget the roadside business?.. it pays more, it's easier (once you get the hang of it you can practically open any car or truck in less than 30 seconds), it's definitely not as dirty and time consuming as a tire change! All of the above are true and, if you can make it on just the lockout biz I say "go for it". But like anything else, it's good to have a back-up plan, and these "free" calls from the auto clubs may keep your financial head above water while you're growing the "lock" part of your new business.

**PLEASE NOTE:

At this time, the following states require locksmith licensing:
Alabama
California
Connecticut
Illinois
Louisiana
Nebraska
Nevada
New Jersey
North Carolina
Oklahoma
Oregon
Tennessee
Texas
Virginia
Washington D.C.

**This does not typically apply to work performed as an Independent Service Provider for the auto clubs (ie: unlocking a vehicle) but may apply to your own Lockout Service business. Some states simply perform a background check while others require you to attend actual classes, online or otherwise. Be sure to check your state and local regulations!

****

THE BASICS

Step 1 : Get your FEIN

When starting a new business you will need to get your Employer Identification Number (USA). It's free and you can apply online at the IRS's website http://www.irs.gov/ . While it may be an option for you to use your Social Security number, I would go ahead and get the EIN and incorporate your business now instead of waiting and having to do it later (once your business has grown to such a point). I started with an LLC only to find out later that I would be better off as an S corporation and pass-through entity for tax purposes. By all means, you will want to talk to a CPA or tax attorney at some point, especially when filing your taxes for the first year. This doesn't have to be expensive and is well worth the time and money spent doing it the right way at the beginning of your venture.

Step 2 : Check Local/State requirements

Check with your state and local revenue departments to ensure you have all of these filings covered as well. Most states will require that you register your business with them and you don't want to find out after the fact that you now owe quite a bit of money in back taxes.

Step 3 : Business Bank account/Accounting

In trying to cover every step required in getting your business off the ground, you'll want to go to your choice of bank and set up a business banking account. This account should be used exclusively for your business purposes: from expenses such as buying tools and paying for insurance and marketing to depositing your cash receipts, credit card receipts and direct deposits from your auto clubs. I would also suggest within this step that you have some sort of accounting software, such as www.QuickBooks.com .

We use QuickBooks online (around $25 per month). Connected to your business bank account, it actually downloads all transactions nightly and sorts them into the accounts where they belong.

It's almost like having an administrative assistant on staff and makes doing taxes at the end of the year that much easier.

You will also need a merchant service account to process your credit cards. We currently have contracted with a veteran-owned and operated company offering our licensees better than average rates. Card swipe plugs into a smart phone and allows you to charge a credit card and email or text a receipt right on the spot. This has also allowed us to do away with the expense of printing invoice books (although you should keep a few actual receipts on hand, as some customers will still request them).

Step 4 : Insurance

With most anything you do in the business world, you're going to want to be properly insured. And these days, there is insurance for almost anything and everything. The last thing you want to do is invest your blood, sweat and tears into a successful business venture, only to have something tragic happen that takes it all away (and possibly more). The auto clubs that you're going to be working with require that you have certain policy coverage. While this is not usually that expensive (typically around $100-$150 a month?), it is required and something you're going to be glad you have if you ever run into any serious problems. While I've never had anything devastating happen, I have used my insurance a handful of times and was happy to have it available.

We have a national account with an insurance agency that will quote all MrQuickPick licensees. They are very familiar with the "Garage Keeper and General Liability" requirements and offer us a discounted rate.

THE AUTO CLUBS

There are approximately a dozen auto clubs for which we are ISP's (Independent Service Providers). MrQuickPick is growing as a national account with each of these clubs and our licensees are given the contact links and step-by-step instructions to quickly and easily sign up to become a new territory service provider.

Are You a Veteran? Military, Police, Fire or First Responder?

****

*GOA stands for "gone on arrival". Sometimes referred to as **CAD (cancelled after dispatched)**, it is when you are given a job but cannot complete it due to member cancelling or no longer on scene when you arrive. Often happens with interstate tire changes and gas deliveries, as DOT (Department of Transportation) monitors major highways and may arrive on scene before you do. Most auto clubs will still pay a GOA service fee, typically smaller but as compensation for your time and mileage. Rules vary as some clubs will not pay GOA if call cancels within 15 minutes of being dispatched or if GOA is as a result of provider arriving past eta (estimated time of arrival).

** Some clubs pay a certain amount per mile as part of your rate agreement. For instance, AAA pays $16.50 per run within 10 miles of your base address. Every mile over the 10 pays an additional $1 per mile. So a job (run) that is 25 miles from your base would pay $16.50 base plus an additional $15 for mileage (total of $31.50). All mileage is verified through a service such as www.mapquest.com and does not include a round trip!

THE SERVICES

Tire changes / Tire plugs

Jump starts / Battery boost

Fuel / Fluid delivery

Lockout service

Light-duty roadside assistance is comprised of the four services listed above. You'll notice that it does not include towing. Towing is another source of revenue that you might consider adding to your business offerings. We just may have doubled our gross revenues by including a tow truck but I personally chose not to go that route due to the additional expenses, insurance liability and what I considered a low return on investment. But there is always a high demand for towing services with the auto clubs, especially during peak seasons. Same goes for locksmith services. Making keys and re-keying lock cylinders can provide a huge boost to your bottom line.

Tire changes "I never said this job would not require SOME hard work"

Tire changes are the most physical of the four services offered. Some vehicles are fairly easy while others can be a real pain. Sometimes they take less than ten minutes and other times closer to an hour. They can always be dangerous! One of the most important things to keep in mind: tire changes can become a damage claim more often than any other service we provide.

What is a damage claim you ask? In a nut shell, a damage claim is when someone "claims you damaged" their vehicle! When you sign up to do contract work for the auto clubs, you agree that any damage you cause to a member's vehicle will be repaired by you. It is very important that you inspect the vehicle upon arrival to ensure there is no pre-existing damage that you could later be blamed for. And since almost every phone now has a camera, it is wise to not only document any pre-existing damage to a member's vehicle but to also take pictures of anything questionable before you proceed with your work.

Our first three years in business had about a dozen damage claims, ranging anywhere from $5 to $700 in repairs. None were serious enough for our liability insurance to kick in, and almost all involved tire changes. These damage claims included anything from a lost lug nut ($5), a broken locking lug nut ($50), broken stud replacement ($40), bent control arm ($250) damaged crank down device ($150) and body damage (to the tune of $700). The body damage was due to the vehicle being raised improperly and then falling off the jack. Easy to do when you get in a hurry and you're not paying attention. By the way, the damage was only $550. The rental car for three days brought it to $700!

I also mentioned tire changes being dangerous. I personally lost part of my thumb by putting it where it didn't belong. Tire changes need to be taken slowly and seriously. A properly done tire change normally takes 10 to 15 minutes from start to finish. Cars are usually pretty easy. SUVs and pickups often require the spare tire to be cranked down from underneath the vehicle, which takes a few extra minutes.

Tire change checklist:

1. Always chock the wheel diagonally opposite the tire you are changing!
2. Put on the emergency brake!
3. Remove the spare tire from the trunk or crank it down from underneath the vehicle prior to raising (jacking)!
4. Check to make sure the spare tire is in good condition. You can waste a lot of time and energy getting all the way to the point of putting the spare on, only to realize the spare is also no good.
5. Loosen the lug nuts while the vehicle is still on the ground. Don't take them all the way off; you don't want to jerk the vehicle around anymore than you have to once it's off the ground.

6. Make sure you have the proper jack and the proper placement. This is a critical part of the entire job. Vehicles have certain "jacking points" or places designed specifically for the jack, and some require a special type of jacking device (such as higher-end sports cars). Always Always Always... if you don't know for sure, refer to the owner's manual. If it comes with a specially designed jacking device, use it! You are allowed to use the jack that comes with the vehicle. Remember, if you cause damage, you will be the one paying for it. And if you pull up on scene and there is already existing damage, you need to make note of it. Take pictures, show the customer, document it somehow. There's nothing like paying for damage that you didn't cause, and that does happen. I've pulled up on jobs where someone had already stripped the lug nuts or had the car fall off the jack. At that point I'm calling the auto club to let them know and have them either take the job back or release me from any liability.
7. Slow down, don't rush! This is not the job to try and make up time with. Pay attention to what you are doing and stay safe.
8. Have the spare tire right there with you when you pull the flat tire off. The less time that vehicle is up on the jack the better.
9. Snug the lug nuts before lowering. Once the vehicle is back on the ground ensure your lug nuts are tight. Loose lug nuts are a large source of damage claims. Not only do tires get damaged but this can also cause accidents and injuries. Check your lug nuts!
10. Don't forget to remove the chock and the emergency brake. I had to return to the scene of a tire change once because I had put the emergency brake on so good that the elderly driver could not release it :-)

Changing a tire on the expressway or other busy road requires extra caution. The vehicle must be far enough off the road to perform the job safely. Use flashers or flares, especially at night. Tow trucks are much better equipped for interstate tire changes therefore we pass on most interstate tire changes.

Tire plugs are another source of revenue, typically paying an extra $12-$15. Here again, the liability increases and one must know what they are doing when plugging a tire. I have had a few experienced drivers that do plugs... otherwise, no on-the-job training!

Jump Starting a vehicle

Providing a jump start or battery boost is normally a quick and painless task. I've had only one damage claim thus far and it was due to pure ignorance. "Jim" thought he would provide an extra service by replacing a corroded battery terminal on a customer's car. Only after cutting off the old terminal and installing the new one did he realize the importance of the 2 inches of cable he had just lopped off. There was no additional "slack" and the cable no longer reached the battery. Result: $160 for a new cable, installed. Aside from that learning experience, it's been quite uneventful. Here again, take your time and pay attention to what you're doing.

Jump Start checklist

1. Always wear eye protection! While I have never had a battery explode on me I've seen one blow up and it goes off like a bomb. Turns out "Norman", the mechanic, was working over the battery with a cigarette in his mouth...enough said.
2. Check (and then double check) the positive and negative terminals. Just because the car has a red cable going to a terminal does not necessarily mean that it was hooked up right in the first place. Typically red is positive and black is negative. Always look for the plus or minus symbol molded onto the battery casing to be sure.
3. Jump box versus "car-to-car". I have heard plenty of stories from my drivers that the box is better and that the "car-to-car" method can mess up your computer brain. I like the box, it's more convenient, especially in tight parking areas. But when my jump box dies, I use my car. I carry a 25 foot, super-heavy duty jumper cable. This allows me to reach the other vehicle from any angle, as

you can't always expect to find an open parking space next to a vehicle in a crowded parking lot (also works well for cars that are parked "nose in" in the garage). I eventually replaced my car battery with a heavier-duty truck battery. I've had no problems using my car and I've had no problems with my brain (although my wife say's that is debatable). Be careful, when using the car-to-car method, about revving the engine while performing the jump start. I have heard that this can blow up the battery. I did have one start smoking on me and I quickly removed and then reinstalled the jumper cables. I will also admit that once, in a big hurry, I myself put the cables on incorrectly and burned my battery up. While it didn't explode, it only lasted for less than a week and it was due to that incorrect procedure.

Fuel or fluid delivery

Sounds very easy and it normally is! Simply take a few gallons of gas to a stranded motorist, pour it in their tank and you're done.

Just a few tidbits on fuel delivery:

1. Diesel fuel and unleaded gas don't mix well. Always use two different containers for unleaded gas and diesel fuel. You don't want to have to pay to have someone's tank flushed.
2. Once again, on the interstate use extreme caution. Many gas deliveries occur on the highway. While quicker than a tire change, you're still only about 6 feet away from some very large trucks flying by at 70+ miles per hour. Be careful!
3. Motorcycles... in my experience, most bikers like to pour their own gas. Can you blame them? Just hand them the gas can and step away from the bike. And always carry a shop rag to wipe off any dripped fuel. Professional, courteous, nice touch!

Unlocking a vehicle

I have found that there are usually three or four different ways to get into a locked vehicle (beside's a brick, which some impatient people still use). Always start with the "least potential for damage" procedure. While we won't go into the specifics of the various methods in detail here (as these are covered in the lockout manual you will get with your tools**) I will touch on some generalities:

1. Don't live or die by the air wedge. While this procedure is fast and will get you into most vehicles, you will eventually run into situations that require other means of entry, such as a knob lifter or "under the window" tool.

2. Always protect the vehicle at the entry point with a paint protector, tape, shop rag, etc.
   Lockouts are the number two source of damage claims (after tire changes). Scratched paint, torn window seals, a few broken door handles, damaged window tint, and yes, even a broken windshield (slap a metal reach rod on a big piece of glass just right and you'll see what I'm talking about). Depending on the type of vehicle, these can be very costly mistakes.

3. Prior to unlocking a vehicle you should record the driver's license information. You really don't want to open that Lexus at the mall for just anyone. Same goes with residential lockouts. You'll want to match up their name on their photo ID with something in their house, such as their mail. Most people appreciate the fact that you're not just opening their home or car to anyone who calls and says they're locked out.

   ** Visit http://www.z-tool.com/Seminar_2.htm for step-by-step auto lockout instruction manuals.

THE TOOLS

Basic Tools required as follows:

Tire changes – don't skimp on the tools required to do a tire change. And don't count on necessarily having the customers jack and tire tools available when you arrive on scene. Most drivers carry a decent 2-ton floor jack and a four-way lug wrench, as well as chocks for the tires and a heavy pair of gloves. Check out these tools at Harbor Freight online:

http://www.harborfreight.com/

Total cost is around $80.00

Jump starts – most drivers carry a jump box (battery booster) and a set of jumper cables. I prefer to carry a high quality, 25 foot long, heavy duty set of jumper cables. This enables me to jump start a car (in a crowded parking lot or garage) without having to worry about being nose to nose or side by side in order to reach the battery.

Total cost: a good jump box can cost anywhere from $60 + and a good set of jumper cables is around $50. The Autozone.com website includes the video "How To Jump Start A Battery".

http://www.autozone.com/

Fuel delivery – you can get a decent 2+ gallon gas can for less than $20. Get a second one if you plan on delivering diesel. Visit www.Kmart.com for both.

Lockouts – I have personally unlocked thousands of vehicles by now and over 95% of them could be opened safely and effectively with a simple air wedge and long reach tool. Steck Manufacturing sells a kit called "The Big Easy" for around $70. They also have a video on their website that shows you how to use it:
http://www.steckmfg.com/video/SteckBigEasyVideo.html

For a more complete lockout kit that will open most any vehicle including semi tractor-trailer's and enable "slim jim" type procedures, I would suggest the Z-tool kit. This kit comes with an up-to-date manual that guides you step-by-step through the unlocking procedure for most vehicles. Their website also offers FREE Online Training Sessions.

Z-Tools web address: http://www.z-tool.com/

If you plan to offer residential and/or commercial lock and lockout services, you can find a wide assortment of these tools at www.Lockpicks.com.

Miscellaneous: other tools you'll want to keep on hand include flashlights, a socket set, assorted wrenches and screwdrivers.

***The light that clips onto your ball cap is a MUST if you're unlocking cars at night... The best $5 you'll ever spend!

Total cost for basic tools to get started: $200- $400

Customers LOVE our New Textable Toll-free Number!

Text your Zip Code and Request to 1-844-ZIP-TEXT

We ❤ 2 TEXT

Question?

Comment!

1-844-ZIP-TEXT

THE MARKETING

Auto Clubs: "Marketing the auto clubs... I thought they were free?" While it's true that we don't pay any fees or advertising costs for the auto club jobs, here are a few tips to "market" your business and yourself to your clubs:

1. Always look and act professional. Wear a nice shirt, preferably with your company name and logo. Dress up if you want, it's your business and reputation! Sometimes I'll unlock a few cars after church on Sunday, still dressed to the nines (not changing any tires mind you). Use car magnets if you don't have a "company car" with lettering. **If you use contractors make sure they have shirts and magnets as well.

2. Take anything and everything the clubs offer you within your agreed territory. Auto clubs score you on different criteria, including what you take and what you turn down. Not saying you should necessarily take the tire change 55 miles away, but definitely don't turn down the jobs in your agreed territory or you will not move up on their "priority" list of who they call first (in fact you may move down).

3. Be on time, or early! The clubs normally will not take an eta (estimated time of arrival) of more than 45 minutes. The better (faster) times you give, the more jobs you can expect. Do your best not to be late. This is another "score" that will move your company up or down on their call list.

4. If a problem arises, fix it! Damage claim, pay issue...whatever might come your way, resolve it to their satisfaction and move on. My experiences with the clubs have been very positive, with very few issues. Touch base with your regional representative every now and then or if you have any questions. They know you are the ones out there in the field and they are usually very "pro" service provider!

**Using contractors: At some point, you may find it helpful or even necessary to use independent contractors. While I started off doing all the work myself, I quickly realized that I could handle a lot more volume (and make a lot more money) hiring others to work my territory with me, eventually expanding to other cities and states. Here is a sample "help wanted" Craigslist ad:

Territory Contractor for Roadside Assistance

"Independent contractors needed to provide light-duty roadside assistance and lockout service in downtown and southside areas. Jump starts, fuel delivery, tire changes and lockouts (vehicle and residential). Residential lock installation. Full and part time available; set your own "on-call" schedule. Reliable vehicle, tools and cell phone required. Excellent compensation, paid weekly. Roadside assistance experience required. Drug screen and background check required. Please reply with your name, city of residence, related experience and phone number with area code. We will contact you with further information".

The Lockout Business: "Out with the old (phonebook) and in with the new (Internet)" Our first phonebook ad was, quite frankly, pretty sad ☹.

We didn't know a thing about advertising and, unfortunately, our phonebook representative didn't either. We ended up with a one-eighth page, $500 month ad and hardly enough calls to justify it, resulting in a terrible ROI. In designing our next phonebook ad, we tried the opposite strategy... all out, full color half-page masterpiece for $1200 a month. Sweet looking ad but, once again, a terrible ROI. Then along came the internet, and marketing this business has completely changed almost overnight!

Internet advertising has leveled the playing field! A great ad in all the phonebooks was VERY costly and required a 12-month contract, something very few start-up companies could swing on a beginner's budget.

But now, phonebooks have shrunk and are practically obsolete. In fact, our business is more cut out for mobile device advertising than most others. The smart phone was practically designed for those needing some type of emergency roadside assistance. Think about it, nearly everyone by now has a smart phone and when people lock their keys in their car, they almost always still have their phone!

I've unlocked many a car that was still running, with a child and/or pet locked inside, but not very often is the cell phone locked in with them (priorities?). And who among us is going to walk back to the customer service desk at the mall or stand in line at the gas station, hoping to find a dusty old phonebook, when you can simply use your smart phone to get quick assistance?

This part of the business has grown exponentially in just the past few years and will continue to do so, as smart phones grow in popularity and availability and decrease in price. Now the challenge is to use this new technology to your advantage, enabling the customer to find and call your business first.

SEO SEM PPC OMG!

In doing research for advertising your business online, you will no doubt run across terms such as SEO (search engine optimization), SEM (search engine marketing) and PPC (pay-per-click). While we use a combination of each, we derive the majority of our lockout business via pay-per-click advertising with Google.

If you are not familiar, Google adwords are the ads that appear at the top of any search page. When someone locks their keys in their car at a mall in Louisville and google's "keys in car", PPC ads will appear at the top of the search screen (PC and smartphone). The goal is to have your high quality, eye catching ad at or near the top of the search screen.

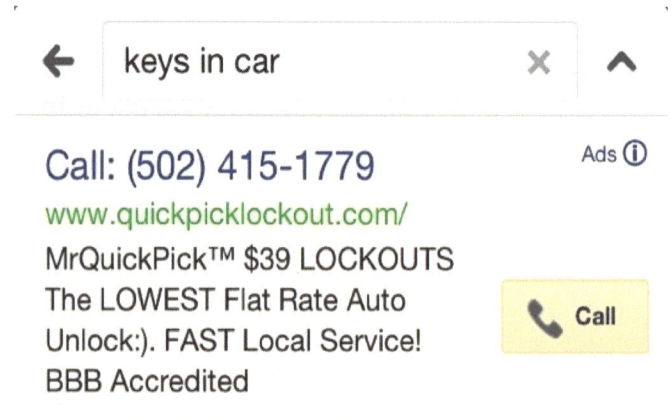

PPC advertising on Google is amazing in that it is customizable in so many ways. From scheduling times and locations to types of ads and cost per click, it is as simple as it can seem complex. And it can be set up and running very quickly...I can set up a brand new city with adwords and start receiving calls in less than 30 minutes (I have done it many, many times)! I can go anywhere, places I have never been and know nothing about and, with adwords and a gps, receive calls from the moment I get there (and shut it down just as quickly and easily when I'm done!).

The challenge is to position your ads as close to the top of the search page as possible, for the least "cost" per click. As stated earlier, marketing will be your biggest expense in the lockout business, so what you spend to make the phone ring can make or break your bottom line. There are so many strategies to running a successful adwords campaign; it is well worth the time and effort to do your homework here or to have a professional set this account up for you.

THE BRAND

As stated earlier, the internet and online marketing has leveled the playing field for many businesses. It has made quality advertising affordable for most everyone and, in the process, caught a lot of "old timers" off guard. I know we were well established online before many of our deeper-pocketed competitors, and while we continue our growth with internet search engines, some are just now starting to play "catch-up".

And while there is an abundance of information on internet marketing techniques and strategies, one thing will set you apart from the rest... your brand name! We have been marketing our name and reputation for quality service from the time we signed up for our EIN. We have always maintained an A+ rating with the Better Business Bureau http://www.bbb.org/louisville/business-reviews/locks-and-locksmiths/quick-pick-lockout-service-llc-in-louisville-ky-159131213 and earned three awards from AAA for providing the best customer service. Your name and your reputation will be the keys to your success!

Unfortunately, for our customers, there are also an abundance of scam artists in this business. "Shell" companies that offer a low price online, only to try the "bait and switch" tactic once they arrive. None of them are members of the BBB or do any work with the auto clubs, and they often don't stay around any one area too long. On the other hand, these scam artists make the great companies like ours (and soon to be yours) stick out in a very positive way. You WILL get word of mouth referrals and repeat business from past customers. All the more reason you should protect your name and reputation.

So will you be just another "Mom & Pop" or a National Brand?

 Hopefully by now you've gained some major insight into this business and possibly made a decision as to whether or not this sounds like the opportunity for you. If you have and it does, we'd like to invite you to join forces with us as a MrQuickPick exclusive territory licensee! It's still your business and you run it completely. The only difference is the brand name! Instead of being the next "Joe Bob's Lockout Service", you'll be licensed to "do business as" (dba) MrQuickPick in your very own exclusive territory, with rights to use all promotional logos and brand name products.

MrQuickPick... "Opening Doors for Entrepreneurs!"

"We are a group of professionals branding together to become the most respected and recognized name in the roadside service industry!"

For complete details visit: http://www.MrQuickPick.com

Email us for more information: info@MrQuickPick.com

Google search LOVES brands and branding!

MrQuickPick's Exclusive Territory Licensing

"What exactly will you get as MrQuickPick?"

First and foremost you're joining the MrQuickPick brand; license to use the name, logos, images, video jingles... anything and everything, including affiliation with our membership and A+ rating with the Better Business Bureau. That's a $35 monthly value in itself!

Second, you are getting an exclusive territory, a specific radius that you and you alone will have the title MrQuickPick (MQP).

You'll receive a MrQuickPick webpage customized with contact info specific to your territory. Calls come **directly to your phone** or our **1-800-391-QUICK** hotline, which then get forwarded to the requested territory licensee.

We also offer assistance setting up the auto clubs and local internet advertising campaigns (Google My Business, Foursquare, Yelp) customized for your exclusive territory, using the MQP brand name and logo/trademarks. Advertising will be consistent across all markets, growing our web presence and brand recognition both locally and nationally.

**Please note: Monthly fee does not include payment of any advertising fees, only the set up and assistance with managing your advertising accounts.

All logo items can be designed and purchased through www.VistaPrint.com with a personalized account for each licensee to order their own custom business cards, shirts, magnets, etc. with MQP logo.

Benefit by getting in early! Joining now allows you the lowest possible fee (* based on territory population).

Finally, we realize that the success of the MQP brand is contingent upon the success of its members … therefore, as a result of joining forces with hundreds of fellow MQP licensees, the sky's the limit with regard to future national marketing opportunities (spokespersons, sponsorships) and additional service offerings like "MrQuickPick Delivers!" and for our veterans: "Vets Unlocking Cars! / Vets Deliver!"

Thanks for the read … we would look forward to working with you!!

Please feel free to contact us with any questions or to check availability of your preferred territory.

Now let's get your business started!

Jon Taylor

MrQuickPick
800.391.QUICK (7842)
Info@MrQuickPick.com

Are You a Veteran?

Retired Military, Police, Fire or First Responder?

Our Customers LOVE our new Textable Toll-free Service Numbers!!

www.ingramcontent.com/pod-product-compliance
Lightning Source LLC
Chambersburg PA
CBHW041142180526
45159CB00002BB/700